ISLINGTON LIBRARIES

3 01

D1352349

ISLING TON

Please return this item on or before the last date stamped below or you may
be liable to overdue charges. To renew an item call the number below, or
access the online catalogue at www.islington.gov.uk/libraries. You will need
your library membership number and PIN number.

17 FEB 2012

16 APR 2012

30 JUL 2012

Res24/9/12

29 OCT 2012

26 MAR 2018

17 OCT 2015

- 4 JUL 2015

Islington Libraries

7 6900   **www.islington.gov.uk/libraries**

Chocolate

WENDY VEALE

JOHN BEAUFOY PUBLISHING

First published in the United Kingdom in 2011 by John Beaufoy Publishing,
11 Blenheim Court, 316 Woodstock Road, Oxford OX2 7NS, England
www.johnbeaufoy.com

10 9 8 7 6 5 4 3 2 1

Copyright © 2011 John Beaufoy Publishing Limited
Copyright © 2011 in text and photographs John Beaufoy Publishing Limited

All rights reserved. No part of this publication may be reproduced, stored in
a retrieval system or transmitted in any form or by any means, electronic,
mechanical, photocopying, recording or otherwise, without the prior written
permission of the publishers and copyright holders.

Great care has been taken to maintain the accuracy of the information
contained in this work. However, neither the publishers nor the author can
be held responsible for any consequences arising from the use of the
information contained therein.

ISBN 978-1-906780-45-6

Project manager: Rosemary Wilkinson
Design: Roger Hammond at bluegum
Photographs: Michael Prior (except p. 70, Ian Garlick)
Front cover photograph: Ian Garlick
Illustration: Stephen Dew

Printed in India by Replika Press Pvt. Ltd.

RECIPE NOTES

✐ Where milk is used in a recipe, this can be full fat, semi-skimmed or skimmed.

✐ All eggs are medium unless otherwise stated.

✐ All spoon measurements are level unless otherwise stated.

✐ Metric and imperial measurements are not always exact equivalents, so only follow one set of measurements within each recipe.

✐ Oven temperatures have been given for conventional electric and gas ovens. For fan ovens, use the following equivalents:

Electricity °C	Electricity (fan) °C
110	90
120	100
130	110
140	120
150	130
160	140
170	150
180	160
190	170
200	180
220	200

Contents

ISLINGTON LIBRARIES	
AL	
3 0120 02493308 7	
Askews & Holts	21-Dec-2011
641.6374	£5.99

Cooking with chocolate

Chocolate has to be the best loved flavour, at least in the western hemisphere. Used as a flavouring ingredient, a drink and as a confectionary, it is hard to imagine a world without the cocoa bean. Unsurprisingly, the scientific name for the Cacao tree is *theobroma cacao* – 'theobroma' meaning 'the food of the gods'!

Did you know?
Chocolate is believed to boost serotonin and endorphin levels in the brain – a feel-good factor.

A 125 g/4½ oz bar of chocolate contains more caffeine than a cup of instant coffee. Other stimulants in chocolate include theobromine. Chocolate increases alertness and gives an instant lift but energy levels are low.

Choosing the perfect chocolate
Choosing the right chocolate for baking or eating could prove confusing: some are smoother than others, some more bitter, sweeter, harder, some are melt-in-the-mouth – the sign of quality chocolate with a

high percentage of cocoa butter which melts just below body temperature – hence it literally does melt in the warmth of the mouth!

More cocoa solids mean a more distinctive chocolate flavour and more cocoa butter gives a smooth, creamy richness to the chocolate.

Some chocolates include other vegetable fats to supplement a lower content of cocoa butter. This not only results in a less distinct flavour but also raises the temperature at which chocolate melts.

Dark or bittersweet chocolate: This is the darkest of all eating chocolates and has a high concentration of cocoa solids and little sugar. It must have a minimum of 35% cocoa solids. Premium brands have 50–55% cocoa solids. The higher the percentage, the more intense the chocolate flavour, but more sugar may be required in baking. There is a semisweet version which has a higher sugar content and is interchangeable with bittersweet chocolate. With good keeping, wrapped and kept in a cool place, it will last a year.

Continental style: This top quality chocolate has a high cocoa butter content of between 32% and 39%. The total cocoa butter and cocoa solids can then be from around 70% and the very bitter version is as high as 90%. With good keeping, wrapped and kept in a cool place, it will last a year.

Milk chocolate: Semi-sweet and with a high cocoa butter content, this chocolate also contains milk. It is difficult to use for baking as it cannot take any moderate heat without burning. It does not store well, so should be wrapped and kept in a cool place but not the fridge as this causes a cloudy 'bloom' on the chocolate.

White chocolate: An imposter really as white chocolate does not contain any cocoa solids but it does contain rich cocoa butter for that creamy taste. Ivory or cream in colour with added sugar and milk, it does not tolerate heat well, so requires gentle handling. It has a short shelf life, so is best stored in the freezer! Choose the continental style (i.e. Belgium) chocolate for best quality.

When the cocoa butter is replaced with other vegetable fats it is no longer white chocolate but a chocolate-flavoured coating.

Chocolate chips, drops or chunks:

Often used as an ingredient in cookies, muffins, cupcakes and for decorations, plain, milk or white chocolate drops are available in small drums or packs and have a shelf life of about 1 year. Store in a cool place.

Chocolate coating or covering:

Once called Cooking Chocolate, this chocolate 'flavour' compound reacts well to heating and does not burn easily as most of if not all the creamy cocoa butter has been replaced with soya bean, palm oil and emulsifiers.

Cocoa powder:

When the cocoa butter is removed from the chocolate liquor, the 'cake' left is processed to cocoa powder. Unsweetened and simple to use, it can be added in place of a couple of tablespoons of flour to chocolate cakes and cookies. And if using a low cocoa solid chocolate in cooking, a couple of teaspoons blended to a paste will add richness.

Drinking chocolate:

Unsweetened cocoa powder blended with milk powder and sugar to make a comforting chocolate drink. Not ideal in cooking. Many low-calorie/low-fat versions are available and also malted chocolate drinks.

Fair Trade label

You can choose to support farmers and their families by buying chocolate with the Fair Trade Certified label which guarantees farmers a minimum price for their cocoa and thus protects their livelihood.

Handling and melting

There are two rules to handling and melting chocolate: do not hurry and do not overheat. For all the care that has been taken from farm to factory to produce your bar of chocolate, simple mistakes at this final stage of sheer enjoyment are often irreversible.

Dark chocolate is much easier to handle, heat and melt than milk or white chocolate with their higher fat content and tendency to burn or 'seize' resulting in a stiff, tacky mess that has to be thrown away. But for all types:

■ Break the chocolate into a heatproof bowl and set over a pan of gently simmering water. Make sure the water is not touching the base of the bowl or that steam cannot escape and be in contact with the chocolate.
■ Take the pan off the heat and leave the chocolate for 5 minutes or so – it will still retain its shape until the last minute – then stir and use as required.
■ If required, cream should be melted with the chocolate, whilst

butter should be added as soon as the chocolate has melted.
■ If making a sauce which contains ingredients with a high water content i.e. fruit juice, these should be added right at the beginning of the melting process.
■ To melt chocolate in a microwave always refer to the manufacturer's instructions as ovens vary considerably. However, as a rule of thumb, break 100 g/4 oz chocolate into a small bowl, then microwave on 'defrost' for 2 minutes depending on the thickness of the bar used. The pieces will appear to remain whole but will have softened all the way through. Stir only occasionally to produce a smooth glossy liquid.
■ A foolproof way of melting or softening chocolate is to place it in a bowl in the airing cupboard overnight!
■ When cooling melted chocolate to be used to cover a cake or for decorations, the chocolate should be left to set in a cool place and not in the fridge as rapid cooling may affect its appearance.

Decorating with chocolate

Use a small, double thickness greaseproof bag for piping chocolate. If the chocolate hardens, simply soften in the piping bag in the microwave or if the opening gets clogged up, just snip off the tip of the bag.

Have chocolate at room temperature, not too cold, when grating, chopping or making large curls.

■ To make chocolate curls (top), melt the chocolate in a small heatproof bowl set over simmering water, then cool for 10 minutes. Spread onto a cold work surface – a slab of marble is ideal. When cold, use a sharp knife almost parallel to the surface and push through the chocolate.

■ Chocolate shavings (middle), are easy to make: use a swivel vegetable peeler along the flat side of a large bar of chocolate, shaving it off in curls.

■ To make chocolate leaves (bottom), brush or coat the underside of clean, unblemished rose or bay leaves with melted chocolate, then leave to set. Peel the leaf away from the chocolate. Store the fragile leaves in an airtight container.

■ To make chocolate triangles (see page 73), melt chocolate in a small bowl set over simmering water, then cool for 10 minutes. Spread onto a piece of baking parchment and when cold, cut into triangles.

Baking tips

Baking tins: Invest in good quality bakeware that will last for years. Loose-bottomed and non-stick tins make for easier removal of fragile cakes and also only require base lining. Spring-form tins are ideal for delicate or fragile recipes – but do make sure they are released carefully once you have eased around the edge with a small palette knife.

Lining cake tins: Use greaseproof or baking parchment paper. Lightly grease the base and sides of the tins before lining, then do the same to the paper. Vegetable oil sprays often used for low-calorie cooking are ideal for this. Line the tins carefully and accurately. Paper creases can spoil the look of the cooked cake.

Cakes that have longer cooking times i.e. fruit cakes will require the base and sides of the tin lining for added protection.

Base-line tins by cutting out a circle of greaseproof paper to fit. If you make cakes on a regular basis, it's worth cutting a number of circles for your most often used tins. Or you can buy ready-cut standard circles.

Dropping consistency: This describes the ideal consistency of the cake mixture – just right to plop off a spoon if gently tapped. Hence if the cake mixture seems dry, add enough milk to form a soft, dropping consistency.

For a flat top: When making a creamed cake mixture make a slight hollow in the centre of the cake before baking. This will then rise in the oven to give a flat top for icing.

For a level top: Use a small flexible palette or butter knife to level off the top of creamed cakes. Do not bang the tin to level as this will knock air out of delicate mixtures.

What went wrong?

Scorching or burning through excessive heat will cause the chocolate to go gritty and it will have a burnt taste. It can easily happen when using the microwave oven to melt chocolate. This is irreversible, so only microwave for very short periods.

Thickening or 'seizing' of a solid mass may be due to uneven heating, the addition of high water content ingredients or steam/water from the saucepan. This is irreversible.

In the oven: Bake cakes on the middle shelf of the preheated oven unless the recipe states otherwise. All ovens are different, so cooking times and temperatures may vary slightly. Check the cake just before the end of cooking time.

To test if a cake is cooked: Insert a skewer or sharp-tipped knife into the centre of the cake – it should come out clean.

Cooling: Allow the cake to cool in the tin for at least 5 minutes before inverting it onto a wire cooling rack. Carefully peel away the paper, then turn the cake the right way up to cool. Ensure the cakes are cold before storing.

Storage: Store cakes in an airtight container. They will keep for a few days.

Freezing cakes: Elaborately decorated cakes should be open frozen until firm, then packed into a rigid container. Stand the cake on a strip of foil or greaseproof paper inside the container, so that it can be lifted out with ease. Label stating 'this way up' to prevent accidental damage. Undo the top of the container before thawing and lift out onto a plate whilst frozen if it will be more difficult to do when thawed.

Rich tea cakes, tea bread, tray bakes, etc can be sliced and separated with paper then reassembled and over-wrapped before freezing. This makes it easy to remove just the required number of slices – ideal for packed lunches.

Meringues are best frozen as undecorated shells. Once defrosted, fill with cream and decorate.

Cooked cheesecakes do not freeze as successfully as uncooked ones and may loose their freshly baked texture.

For best results always leave the cakes to defrost at room temperature. Allow 5–6 hours, or overnight.

A 'bloom' on the chocolate – whitish, mottled spots – can be due to a number of reasons, such as rapid cooling in the fridge, moisture from the steam when melting over a pan of water or the addition of ingredients which do not mix well with the chocolate. Whilst still edible, the appearance of the chocolate is spoilt.

I

cakes &
tray bakes

Makes 24
Prep time: 10 mins
Cook time: 25–30 mins

175 g/6 oz butter
175 g/6 oz caster sugar
3 eggs

175 g/6 oz self-raising flour
1 tsp baking powder
100 g/3½ oz ready-to-eat apricots, chopped
100 g/3½ oz good quality white chocolate, chopped
1 tbsp icing sugar, sieved

Apricot & white chocolate tray bake

1 Grease and line a 30 x 20 cm/12 x 8 in tray bake tin. Preheat the oven to 180°C/350°F/Gas 4.

2 In a mixing bowl, cream the butter and sugar together until light and fluffy. Beat in the eggs, flour and baking powder.

3 Mix in the apricots and white chocolate. Spread evenly into the tin and bake for 25–20 minutes or until firm to the touch and golden.

4 Cool in the tin for 5 minutes before turning out onto a wire rack to cool completely. Dust with icing sugar and cut into fingers.

TIP
Replace the apricots with dried apple and the white chocolate with dark chocolate.

Makes 8–10 slices
Prep time: 15 mins
Cook time: 50 mins–1 hour

225 g/8 oz butter
225 g/8 oz caster sugar

4 eggs, beaten
a few drops of vanilla extract
225 g/8 oz self-raising flour
1 tbsp cocoa powder
100 g/3½ oz plain chocolate

Chocolate marble slice

1 Grease and line a 900 g/2 lb loaf tin. Preheat the oven to 180°C/350°F/Gas 4.

2 In a mixing bowl, cream together the butter and sugar until light and fluffy, then gradually beat in the eggs and vanilla. Fold in the flour.

3 Transfer half the mixture to another bowl. Sift and fold the cocoa powder into this portion.

4 Break the chocolate into a small heatproof bowl and set over a pan of barely simmering water. Stir until the chocolate melts. Leave to cool slightly, then fold into the chocolate mixture.

5 Put alternative spoonfuls of the chocolate and plain mixtures into the loaf tin. Use a knife to swirl together creating a marbled effect.

6 Bake for 50 minutes–1 hour or until well risen and firm to the touch. Turn out onto a wire rack to cool. Serve sliced.

VARIATION
Add the finely grated zest of 1 lemon or 1 orange or chopped stem ginger to the plain sponge mix. For a spicy note add ½ tsp ground cinnamon to the chocolate sponge mix.

Makes 14 slices
Prep time: 30 mins
Cook time: 1–1¼ hours

200 g/7 oz dark chocolate (min. 70–75% cocoa solids)
200 g/7 oz butter, cubed
1 tbsp instant coffee granules
85 g/3 oz self-raising flour
85 g/3 oz plain flour
¼ tsp bicarbonate of soda
400 g/14 oz light soft brown sugar

3 tbsp cocoa powder
3 eggs, beaten
5 tbsp buttermilk or soured cream

GANACHE
200 g/7 oz dark chocolate (min. 70–75% cocoa solids), chopped
50 g/1¾ oz butter
284 ml/10 fl oz carton double cream
2 tbsp caster sugar
white and dark chocolate curls (see page 11), to decorate

The ultimate chocolate cake

1 Grease and line a 20 cm/7 in deep, round, loose-bottomed cake tin. Preheat the oven to 160°C/325°F/Gas 3.

2 Break the chocolate into a medium saucepan together with the butter and coffee. Add 125 ml/4 fl oz boiling water. Warm through over a low heat, stirring until melted and smooth.

3 Put all the dry ingredients into a large bowl. Make a well in the centre and add the eggs and milk or cream. Pour on the warm chocolate and mix to a smooth batter. Pour into the cake tin and bake for 1–1¼ hours or until a skewer inserted in the centre comes out clean. Leave to cool in the tin, then turn out onto a wire rack to cool completely. Cut into 3 horizontal layers.

4 To make the ganache, place the chocolate and butter in a mixing bowl. Heat the cream and sugar together in a saucepan and when just scalding, pour onto the chocolate. Cover and leave for a few minutes, then stir until smooth and glossy.

5 Sandwich the layers together with some of the ganache, then pour the rest over the cake. Decorate with chocolate curls.

Serves 8–10
Prep time: 25 mins
Cook time: 1¹/₄ hours

225 g/8 oz self-raising flour
40 g/1¹/₂ oz cocoa powder
1 level tbsp baking powder
¹/₂ tsp salt
2 large eggs
175 ml/6 fl oz semi-skimmed milk
75 g/2³/₄ oz caster sugar

100 g/3¹/₂ oz butter, melted
250 g/9 oz firm dessert plums, stoned and finely chopped

TOPPING
25 g/1 oz butter
75 g/2³/₄ oz self-raising flour
75 g/2³/₄ oz demerara sugar
50 g/1³/₄ oz chopped toasted hazelnuts
25 g/1 oz good quality white or milk chocolate chips

Chocolate streusel cake

1 Grease and line a 20 cm/8 in spring-form cake tin. Preheat the oven to 190°C/375°F/Gas 5.

2 Place the flour, cocoa powder, baking powder and salt into a large bowl.

3 In another large bowl whisk together the eggs, milk and sugar, then whisk in the melted butter.

4 Sift the dry ingredients onto the egg mixture and swiftly fold in, together with the plums. Don't worry if the mixture looks lumpy; it must not be over-stirred. Spoon into the tin.

5 For the topping, rub the butter into the flour to resemble breadcrumbs, then stir in the sugar and hazelnuts with 1 tbsp cold water to form a rough crumble. Scatter over the cake.

6 Bake for 1¹/₄ hours until risen and springy. (Cover the tin with foil if the cake darkens too quickly). As soon as it is ready, scatter on the chocolate chips. Leave to cool in the tin for 30 minutes before transferring to a wire rack to cool completely.

Serves 8
Prep time: 3–5 mins
Cook time: 25–35 mins

175 g/6 oz self-raising flour
25 g/1 oz cocoa powder
1 rounded tsp baking powder
125 g/4½ oz caster sugar
150 ml/5 fl oz groundnut oil

150 ml/5 fl oz semi-skimmed milk
2 eggs

BUTTER FILLING
25 g/1 oz cocoa powder
175 g/6 oz butter, softened
225 g/8 oz icing sugar + 1 tsp
a few drops vanilla extract

Five minute chocolate wonder

1 Grease and base-line 2 x 18 cm/7 in sandwich tins. Preheat the oven to 160°C/325°F/Gas 3.

2 Place all the ingredients for the cake in a food processor and blend together. When the mixture becomes smooth, dark and creamy, divide it between the 2 tins.

3 Bake for 25–35 minutes or until risen. Turn out onto wire racks to cool.

4 For the butter filling, mix the cocoa powder to a paste with a very little hot water. Leave to cool. Cream the butter in a bowl. Sift in the 225 g/8 oz icing sugar and a few drops of vanilla extract. Whisk really well until pale in colour and fluffy, then beat in the cocoa paste.

5 Sandwich the cooled cakes together with the butter filling. Sprinkle the top with a dusting of icing sugar.

Makes 9 squares
Prep time: 20 mins
Cook time: 1–1½ hours

250 g/9 oz plain flour
2 level tsp ground ginger
2 level tsp baking powder
1 level tsp bicarbonate of soda
50 g/1¾ oz cocoa powder

175 g/6 oz medium oatmeal
175 g/6 oz unsalted butter
175 g/6 oz dark soft brown sugar
300 g/10½ oz golden syrup
300 ml/10 fl oz semi-skimmed milk
1 egg, beaten
85 g/3 oz dark chocolate (min. 50–55% cocoa solids), chopped

Chocolate & ginger parkin

1 Grease and base-line a 23 cm/9 in square, deep cake tin. Preheat oven to 180°C/350°F/Gas 4.

2 Sieve the first 5 dry ingredients together into a large bowl. Stir in the oatmeal.

3 Meanwhile gently heat together the butter, sugar and syrup in a saucepan until the sugar has dissolved. Whisk in the milk and egg, then beat into the dry ingredients, combining well to a smooth thick batter.

4 Fold in the chocolate. Pour into the tin and bake for 1–1½ hours or until firm to the touch but still slightly moist in the middle when tested with the point of a knife. Leave to cool in the tin before turning out onto a wire rack to cool completely.

Makes 9 squares

Prep time: 20 mins

Cook time: 1¼ hours

225 g/8 oz butter, softened

175 g/6 oz soft light brown sugar

1 tsp vanilla extract

3 large eggs

425 ml/15 fl oz unsweetened chunky apple sauce

225 g/8 oz self-raising flour

50 g/1¾ oz ground almonds

100 g/3½ oz cocoa powder

1 tsp baking powder

1 tsp ground ginger or cinnamon

175 g/6 oz dark chocolate (min. 50%–55% cocoa solids), chopped

Spiced chocolate applesauce cake

1 Grease and line a 20 cm/8 in deep, square cake tin. Preheat the oven to 180°C/350°F/Gas 4.

2 Cream the butter and sugar together until light and fluffy, then beat in the vanilla and eggs. Fold in the apple sauce.

3 Sift the flour, ground almonds, cocoa powder, baking powder and spice onto the applesauce mix and carefully fold in, finally adding the chopped chocolate.

4 Spoon into the cake tin and bake for 1¼ hours or until a skewer inserted into the centre comes out clean. Leave to cool in the tin for 10 minutes before transferring to a wire rack to cool completely.

TIP

To make your own apple sauce, peel, core and dice 4 Bramley apples. Place in a pan with 1–2 tbsp caster sugar and 1–2 tbsp water. Cover and cook gently for 10 mins or until soft.

Serves 10–12
Prep time: 30 mins
Cook time: 40 mins

The alternative Christmas chocolate cake

100 g/3¹/₂ oz dark chocolate (min. 70–75% cocoa solids)

150 ml/5 fl oz soured cream

175 g/6 oz unsalted butter

300 g/10¹/₂ oz soft brown sugar

zest of 2 oranges

3 eggs, beaten

300 g/10¹/₂ oz plain flour

2 tbsp cocoa powder

¹/₂ tsp baking powder

1¹/₂ tsp bicarbonate of soda

FILLING

300 g/10¹/₂ oz fresh cranberries

juice of 2 oranges

125 g/4¹/₂ oz caster sugar

FROSTING

2 egg whites

350 g/12 oz caster sugar

a good pinch of salt

juice of 1 lemon

¹/₂ tsp cream of tartar

DECORATION

foil-wrapped chocolate coins

whole physalis

cocoa powder, to dust

1 Grease and line a 23 cm/9 in spring-form cake tin. Preheat the oven to 180°C/350°F/Gas 4.

2 Heat the chocolate in a bowl set over a pan of gently simmering water. Remove from the pan and leave to cool a little. Stir in the soured cream.

continued next page

3 In a large bowl cream together the butter and brown sugar until pale and fluffy. Whisk in the orange zest, then the eggs, a little at a time, followed by the cooled chocolate and cream.

4 Sift on the remaining dry ingredients. Gently fold through to form a smooth batter. Pour into the tin and bake for 40 minutes or until risen and a skewer inserted into the centre comes out clean. Leave in the tin for 10 minutes before turning out onto a wire rack to cool.

5 Meanwhile make the filling: simmer the cranberries with the orange juice until the cranberries have softened and most of the fruit juice has evaporated. Stir in the sugar, leave to cool, then chill.

6 Now make the frosting: place all the ingredients in a large, grease-free bowl. Add 1 tablespoon of water. Set over a pan of gently simmering water and whisk with electric beaters for 10 minutes or until smooth and light. Remove from the pan and leave to cool, then cover with cling film until ready to use.

7 Split the chocolate cake in half horizontally and prick the lower half with a skewer. Spread the cranberries evenly over this and top with the other half.

8 Spread the frosting liberally over the top and sides of the cake. Leave to harden slightly, then decorate with coins and fruit and dust with cocoa powder.

Makes 8 slices
Prep time: 15 mins
Cook time: 40–45 mins

175 g/6 oz butter
175 g/6 oz caster sugar
zest and juice of 2 oranges
2 tbsp milk

3 eggs
175 g/6 oz self-raising flour
1 tsp baking powder
75 g/2¾ oz good quality white chocolate, roughly chopped
½ tsp ground cinnamon (optional)
3 tbsp granulated sugar

White chocolate & orange drizzle cake

1 Grease and line a 900 g/2 lb loaf tin. Preheat the oven to 180°C/350°F/Gas 4.

2 In a large bowl cream together the butter, sugar and orange zest until light and fluffy. Whisk in the milk, then gradually beat in the eggs, one at a time with a spoonful of flour.

3 Fold in the remaining flour, baking powder, chocolate pieces and cinnamon, if liked.

4 Spoon into the tin, levelling the surface and bake for 40–45 minutes until well risen, golden and a skewer inserted into the centre comes out clean.

5 Meanwhile make the syrup: place the orange juice in a small saucepan and bring to the boil until reduced to 3 tablespoons. Leave to cool. Gently stir in the granulated sugar until it is just starting to absorb the juice and dissolve.

6 As soon as the cake comes out of the oven, prick it with a skewer several times and drizzle over the orange syrup. Leave the cake in the tin to cool completely before turning out.

Serves 8–10
Prep time: 15 mins
Cook time: 30–40 mins

100 g/3½ oz butter, diced
125 g/4½ oz dark chocolate
(min. 70–75 % cocoa solids)

6 eggs, separated
a pinch of salt
6 tbsp caster sugar
150 g/5½ oz ground almonds
whole almonds, to decorate
cocoa powder or icing sugar, for dusting

Sunken gluten-free chocolate cake

1 Grease and base-line a 23 cm/9 in spring-form cake tin. Preheat the oven to 160°C/325°F/Gas 3.

2 Melt the butter and chocolate together in a large, heatproof bowl set over a pan of gently simmering water. Remove from the pan and beat until smooth. Leave to cool for 5 minutes, then beat in the egg yolks.

3 In a large clean bowl whisk the egg whites with a pinch of salt until soft peaks form. Continue whisking, adding in the sugar 1 tablespoon at a time, until the whites become stiff. Stir 2 tablespoons of this into the chocolate mixture and stir in the ground almonds, then carefully fold in the remainder of the egg whites.

4 Dust the sides of the cake tin with a little cocoa powder to help prevent sticking, then spoon in the mixture. Bake for 30–40 minutes or until well risen and just firm to touch. Cool in the tin.

5 When ready to serve, decorate with whole almonds and dust liberally with cocoa powder or icing sugar.

2

cookies,
buns & bars

Makes 12
Prep time: 15 mins
Cook time: 20 mins plus chilling

200 g/7 oz self-raising flour
200 g/7 oz soft light brown sugar
6 tbsp cocoa powder, sieved
150 ml/5 fl oz sunflower or
groundnut oil

300 ml/10 fl oz carton soured cream
2 eggs
100 g/3½ oz dark chocolate (min.
50–55% cocoa solids), finely
chopped
200 g/7 oz good quality white or milk
chocolate, broken into pieces
3 tbsp caster sugar, to taste
milk chocolate shavings (see page
11), to decorate

Chocolate cupcakes

1 Line a 12-hole muffin tin with deep paper cases. Preheat
the oven to 180°C/350°F/Gas 4.

2 In a large bowl mix together the flour, sugar, cocoa powder,
sunflower or groundnut oil, 150 ml/5 fl oz of the soured
cream and the eggs together with 6 tablespoons cold water.
Whisk to combine all the ingredients to a smooth batter.

3 Stir in the dark chocolate. Carefully divide the mixture
between the paper cases and bake for 20 minutes or until
risen and firm to the touch. Transfer to a wire rack to cool.

4 Meanwhile make the icing: gently heat together the white or
milk chocolate, remaining soured cream and caster sugar in a
bowl over a pan of simmering water. Stir until smooth. Cool,
cover and chill the icing until firm enough to swirl on top of
the cupcakes, then decorate with the chocolate shavings.

TIP
Finely chop the dark
chocolate in a food
processor or use
chocolate chips for
ease.

Makes 16 squares
Prep time: 15 mins
Cook time: 30–40 mins

175 g/6 oz dark chocolate (min.
70–75% cocoa solids)
175 g/6 oz butter
3 eggs, beaten

200 g/7 oz caster sugar
a few drops natural vanilla extract
85 g/3 oz self-raising flour
25 g/1 oz cocoa powder + extra for
dusting
75 g/2¾ oz whole walnuts or pecan
nuts, coarsely chopped

Boston brownies

1 Lightly grease and line a 20 cm/8 in square baking tin,
5 cm/2 in deep, with parchment paper allowing a paper
collar 2.5 cm/1 in above the tin. Preheat the oven to
160°C/325°F/Gas 3.

2 Melt the chocolate and butter together in a large heatproof
bowl set over a pan of simmering water.

3 Remove the bowl from the heat and briskly stir in all the
remaining ingredients until well blended. Pour into the tin,
then bake for 30–40 minutes or until springy to the touch but
slightly soft in the centre.

4 Leave to cool in the tin for 2 hours, then turn out onto a
board. Cut into squares and dust with cocoa powder.

VARIATIONS
■ Replace the nuts with chunks of white chocolate for a really
decadent brownie.
■ For a thoroughly adult brownie, soak 50 g/2 oz pitted
prunes in brandy overnight, then fold in with chopped
almonds instead of walnuts at stage 3.

Makes 16
Prep time: 15 mins
Cook time: 40 mins

175 g/6 oz dark chocolate
(min. 50–55% cocoa solids)
175 g/6 oz unsalted butter
225 g/8 oz light soft brown sugar

3 large eggs, beaten
85 g/3 oz plain flour
50 g/1¾ oz cocoa powder
½ tsp baking powder
200 g/7 oz full-fat cream cheese
a few drops of vanilla extract
1 tbsp icing sugar

Chocolate cheesecake swirls

1 Grease and base-line an 18 cm/7 in square baking tin,
5 cm/2 in deep. Preheat the oven to 180°C/350°F/Gas 4.

2 Gently melt together the chocolate, butter and brown sugar
in a large saucepan over a moderate heat. Stir until all
ingredients are smooth. Remove from the heat, leave to cool
slightly, then whisk in the eggs. Keep whisking until the
mixture is smooth.

3 Sift on the flour, cocoa powder and baking powder, folding
into the mixture. Pour into the tin.

4 Beat together the cream cheese, vanilla extract and icing
sugar. Dollop small spoonfuls over the chocolate mix then,
using a rounded knife, swirl the cream cheese through to
create a marbled effect.

5 Bake for 40 minutes or until just firm. Cool in the tin
before marking into squares.

Makes approx. 30
Prep time: 20 mins
Cook time: 8–12 mins

225 g/8 oz butter
125 g/4½ oz soft brown sugar
125 g/4½ oz caster sugar
2 eggs

a few drops vanilla extract
325 g/11½ oz plain flour
1 tsp bicarbonate of soda
½ tsp baking powder
200 g/7 oz dark chocolate (min. 50–55% cocoa solids), chopped or chocolate chips

Chocolate chip cookies

1 Lightly grease 2 baking sheets. Preheat the oven to 190°C/375°F/Gas 5.

2 In a large bowl, cream the butter and sugars together until light, pale and fluffy, then gradually beat in the eggs and vanilla extract.

3 Sift in the flour, bicarbonate of soda and baking powder, then add the chocolate. Using a rubber spatula, work all the ingredients together to a pliable dough.

4 To bake straightaway, shape the dough into 30 walnut-sized balls and place well-spaced on the baking sheets. Use a fork to gently press down each ball. Bake for 10 minutes or until the centres are just firm to the touch. Transfer to a wire rack to cool. Serve warm or cold.

5 To bake as required, split the dough in half, roll each out into a sausage shape approx. 5 cm/2 in in diameter, wrap in cling film and refrigerate until required. When required, simply slice into 2 cm/¾ in thick cookies, space out on a baking sheet and bake as above.

Makes 20
Prep time: 20 mins
Cook time: 50–60 mins

2 egg whites
50 g/1¾ oz caster sugar
50 g/1¾ oz icing sugar, sieved
2 level tbsp cocoa powder, sieved,
plus extra for dusting

FILLING
250 ml/9 fl oz whipping cream
1 tbsp icing sugar, sieved
75 g/2¾ oz dark or white chocolate,
finely grated

Chocolate kisses

1 Line 2 baking sheets with parchment. Preheat the oven to
140°C/275°F/Gas 1.

2 Whisk the egg whites in a clean bowl until they form soft
peaks. Very gradually whisk in the caster sugar, icing sugar
and cocoa powder until the meringue is really stiff and dry.

3 Spoon or pipe small whirls onto the baking sheets. Bake
for 50–60 minutes or until dry and crisp. Turn the
meringues over and leave in the turned-off oven to cool
completely. Store in an airtight container until required.

4 When ready to serve, whisk the cream until just stiffening,
then fold in the icing sugar and grated chocolate. Spoon a
small dollop of the cream onto half of the meringues, then
add the remaining halves and press lightly together. Dust
lightly with cocoa powder.

TIP
Do not sandwich
the meringues until
just ready to serve as
they will soften.

Makes 12
Prep time: 20 mins plus resting
Cook time: 12–15 mins

150 g/5½ oz icing sugar
3 rounded tbsp cocoa powder

150 g/5½ oz ground almonds or hazelnuts
3 egg whites
50 g/1¾ oz caster sugar
a few drops of vanilla extract

Chocolate macaroons

1 Line 2 large baking sheets with parchment. Preheat the oven to 160°C/325°F/Gas 3.

2 Make a stencil for the meringues by dipping the rim of a 4 cm/2 in pastry cutter in flour, then gently tapping onto the baking sheets. Mark out 12 circles, 2.5 cm/1 in apart.

3 Blend the icing sugar, cocoa powder and nuts in a food processor until very fine.

4 In a large clean bowl, whisk the egg whites until soft peaks form. Gradually add the caster sugar, whisking until the meringue is stiff and glossy. Fold in the ground nut mixture and the vanilla extract.

5 Gently spoon into a large disposable piping bag, snip off the bottom to make a 1 cm/¾ in hole, then pipe into rounds using the flour circles as a guide. Give the baking sheets a sharp rap to eliminate any air bubbles and leave to 'set' in a cool dry place for 30 minutes.

6 Bake one sheet at a time for 12–15 minutes or until they feel just firm, risen and glossy with a bubbled rim around the base. Cool on the sheets before carefully removing from the parchment paper.

Makes approx. 30
Prep time: 30 mins plus cooling
Suitable for freezing

250 g/9 oz dark chocolate (min.
70–75% cocoa solids)
150 ml/5 fl oz double cream

75 g/2¾ oz unsalted butter
2 tbsp rum or brandy
50 g/1¾ oz cocoa powder mixed
with a little icing sugar, for dusting
30–36 white paper sweet cases
(optional)

Rocky chocolate truffles

1 Gently melt the chocolate with the cream and butter in a
heatproof bowl set over a pan of simmering water.

2 Remove from the heat and stir in the rum or brandy. Beat
well until the mixture is shiny and smooth. Leave to cool
completely, cover and refrigerate for 3–4 hours or until the
mixture has firmed up enough to shape into truffles.

3 Have the paper cases ready on a tray or plate, if using. Sift
the cocoa powder and icing sugar onto a plate. Scoop half a
heaped teaspoon of truffle mix and toss into the cocoa powder
mix, then spoon into a case.

4 Store in the fridge for up to 3 days. They also freeze well.

VARIATION
For smooth, round truffles, dust your hands with cocoa
powder, then roll the mix into a small ball, roll it in the cocoa
powder and icing sugar, then place in a case. Work as quickly
as possible and do not over-roll the truffles.

Makes 12–16
Prep time: 10 mins
Cook time: 20–25 mins

225 g/8 oz butter
150 g/5½ oz light soft brown sugar
75 g/2¾ oz desiccated coconut
75 g/2¾ oz dried blueberries

50 g/1¾ oz cornflake cereal
2 tbsp cocoa powder
150 g/5½ oz self-raising flour
150 g/5½ oz white chocolate, broken into pieces
150 g/5½ oz dark chocolate (min. 50–55% cocoa solids), broken into pieces

Chocolate, coconut & blueberry cereal bars

1 Base-line a 15 x 25 x 2.5 cm/6 x 10 x 1 in baking tin. Preheat the oven to 180°C/350°F/Gas 4.

2 In a large saucepan, melt the butter over a low heat. Stir in the sugar, coconut, blueberries and cornflakes. Gradually sift in the cocoa powder and flour. Mix together well.

3 Turn into the tin and level with a knife. Bake for 20–25 minutes. Leave in the tin, then cut into bars whilst still warm.

4 Meanwhile, melt the white and dark chocolate separately in heatproof bowls set over pans of simmering water. Spoon the melted plain chocolate in thick lines over the top of the tray bake, then fill in the gaps with the melted white chocolate. Use a palette knife to swirl the chocolates together to create a marbled effect. When the chocolate has just set, cut again into bars. Allow to cool completely before transferring to an airtight container.

Makes 32 small cookies
Prep time: 20 mins
Cook time: 10–15 mins

225 g/8 oz unsalted butter, softened
150 g/5½ oz golden granulated sugar plus extra for topping
1 egg

300 g/10½ oz plain flour
1 tsp baking powder
1 tsp cream of tartar
100 g/3½ oz white chocolate, chopped (or chocolate chips)
100 g/3½ oz dried cranberries
100 g/3½ oz pistachio nuts, coarsely chopped

White chocolate, cranberry & pistachio cookies

1 Line 2 baking sheets with parchment paper. Preheat the oven to 190°C/375°F/Gas 5.

2 Cream the butter and sugar together in a large bowl until light, pale and fluffy, then beat in the egg.

3 Sift in the flour, baking powder and cream of tartar. Use a wooden spoon to combine well, then fold in the white chocolate, cranberries and nuts. If the dough seems sticky, sift in a little more flour.

4 Roughly shape the dough into small walnut-sized balls and space evenly apart on the baking sheets. Dip the prongs of a fork into cold water, then into granulated sugar and lightly press cookies into rounds.

5 Bake for 10–15 minutes or until tinged golden brown yet still slightly soft. Leave to cool on the baking sheet for a few minutes, then transfer to a cooling rack to cool completely.

Makes 20–24 small squares
Prep time: 15 mins
Cook time: 35 mins plus cooling

225 g/8 oz plain flour
75 g/2¾ oz caster sugar
150 g/5½ oz cold unsalted butter, diced

CARAMEL LAYER
125 g/4½ oz unsalted butter
125 g/4½ oz light soft brown sugar
1 x 397 g can condensed milk
a few drops of vanilla extract

CHOCOLATE TOPPING
200 g/7 oz dark or milk chocolate
1 tbsp vegetable oil

Millionaire's shortbread

1 Grease and base-line an 18 cm/7 in square cake tin,
5 cm/2 in deep. Preheat the oven to 180°C/350°F/Gas 4.

2 Mix together the flour and sugar in a large bowl. Rub in the
cold butter until it resembles breadcrumbs, then knead the
mixture to a smooth dough. Press the dough evenly into the
tin. Prick all over with a fork. Bake for 20–25 minutes until
light golden brown. Leave to cool.

3 For the caramel layer, melt the butter and sugar in a small
pan over a gentle heat. Add the condensed milk. Stirring
constantly, allow the mixture to come to a steady gentle simmer
for 5 minutes. Remove from the heat, beat in the vanilla extract
and pour over the shortbread. Leave to cool.

4 Melt the chocolate in a heatproof bowl set over a pan of
simmering water. Stir in the vegetable oil, then spread over
the cold caramel. Chill in the fridge until set. Cut into squares
to serve.

VARIATION
Stir a handful of raisins or sultanas into the caramel topping.

3

desserts &
indulgences

Serves 8

Prep time: 25 mins plus freezing

Cook time: 20 mins

125 g/4½ oz butter

125 g/4½ oz caster sugar

2 eggs

75 g/2¾ oz self-raising flour

25 g/1 oz cocoa powder

FILLING

2 tbsp kirsch, Grand Marnier or Tia Maria, to taste

450 g/1 lb ricotta cheese

2 tbsp icing sugar, to sweeten

120 ml/4 fl oz very strong cold black coffee

100 g/3½ oz dark chocolate (min. 70–75% cocoa solids) chopped

100 g/3½ oz white chocolate, chopped

50 g/1¾ oz toasted flaked almonds

50 g/1¾ oz glacé cherries, roughly chopped

½ x 397 g/14 oz can black cherries, drained and pitted

cocoa powder, to dust

Choc-cherry spectacular

1 You will need one 19 cm/7 in and one 20 cm/8 in round sandwich tin plus one 19 cm/7 in glass pudding bowl. Line the bowl with cling film. Preheat the oven to 190°C/375°F/Gas 5.

2 Cream the butter and sugar until light and fluffy. Beat in the eggs 1 at a time, then sift and fold in the flour and cocoa powder. Add a little milk if needed to make a soft, dropping consistency.

3 Divide the mixture between the 2 tins and level. Bake for 20–25 minutes or until risen and springy to the touch. Cool a little, then turn out. Roll out the larger sponge to make it a little thinner. Use this sponge while still warm to line the pudding bowl. Sprinkle over your chosen liqueur.

4 Mix together the ricotta and enough sugar to sweeten. Loosen with the coffee, then fold in the remaining ingredients. Spoon into the bowl, place the second sponge on top and press down firmly with a weighted dessert plate. Freeze for 3 hours, bringing out 1 hour before serving, dusted with cocoa powder.

Serves 8–10

Prep time: 40 mins plus chilling

Cook time: 20 mins

4 egg whites

250 g/9 oz caster sugar

1 tsp cornflour

1 tsp white wine vinegar

2 tsp coffee granules dissolved in
1 tbsp boiling water

FILLING

200 g/7 oz dark chocolate
(min. 70–75% cocoa solids),
broken into small pieces

600 ml/1 pt double cream

2 tbsp coffee liqueur or brandy

1 tbsp icing sugar

sifted cocoa powder, to decorate

Mocha mallow roulade

1 Line a 30 x 20 cm/12 x 8 in Swiss roll tin with baking
parchment. Preheat the oven to 160°C/325°F/Gas 3.

2 Whisk the egg whites until stiff, then whisk in the caster
sugar 1 tbsp at a time until stiff and shiny. Fold in the
cornflour, vinegar and coffee, then spread gently into the
tin. Bake for 20 minutes or until the surface is just crisp.

3 Leave to cool in the tin for a few minutes. Dust a piece of
parchment paper slightly larger than the tin with icing sugar.
Tip the meringue onto the paper, then ease away the lining.

4 Melt the chocolate in a heatproof bowl set over gently
simmering water. Remove from the heat and leave to cool.
Whip the cream and divide between 2 bowls. Reserve 5 tbsp
of the chocolate, then fold the rest into 1 bowl of cream.
Spread this over the roulade almost to the edges. Fold the
liqueur and icing sugar into the other bowl and spread on top.

5 Starting from one short side, roll up the meringue. Place
on a tray, seal side down, and refrigerate overnight to firm.
To serve melt the reserved chocolate. Dust the roulade with
cocoa powder, then drizzle over the chocolate.

Serves 6–8
Prep time: 20 mins
Cook time: 15–20 mins

50 g/1¾ oz cocoa powder
150 g/5 oz organic dried apricots,
chopped
200 ml/7 fl oz boiling water
a few drops of vanilla extract
1 tsp bicarbonate of soda
75 g/2¾ oz unsalted butter

125 g/4½ oz light muscovado sugar
2 eggs
175 g/6 oz self-raising flour

CHOC-ORANGE SAUCE
175 g/6 oz soft brown sugar
75 g/2¾ oz unsalted butter
zest & juice of 1 orange
100 g/3½ oz dark chocolate (min.
50–55% cocoa solids)
150 ml/5 fl oz double cream

Chocolate icky sticky
with choc-orange sauce

1 Lightly grease eight 150 ml/5 fl oz pudding basins and dust
with cocoa powder. Preheat the oven to 190°C/375°F/Gas 5.

2 Put the apricots in a bowl and pour over the boiling water.
Add the vanilla and bicarbonate of soda and leave to one side.

3 Cream the butter and sugar together in a mixing bowl until
light and fluffy. Gradually beat in the eggs, then add the flour,
the remaining cocoa powder and the apricot mixture. Mix
well. At this stage the mixture is very sloppy.

4 Pour the mixture into the basins and bake for
15-20 minutes or until the tops are set and the puddings have
risen and shrunk from the sides. Turn out of the basins onto
individual serving plates.

5 Meanwhile put all the sauce ingredients in a pan and heat
gently, stirring occasionally, until the sugar is dissolved. Pour
over the puddings.

Serves 6–8
Prep time: 25 mins
Cook time: 45–55 mins

250 g/9 oz butter
50 g/1³/₄ oz demerara sugar
6 whole blanched almonds
3 pears, peeled, halved & cored
175 g/6 oz caster sugar
2 large eggs

125 g/4¹/₂ oz self-raising flour
2 tbsp cocoa powder
50 g/1³/₄ oz ground almonds
2 tbsp milk

MILK CHOCOLATE SAUCE
75 g/2³/₄ oz milk chocolate (min. 50–55% cocoa solids), broken in pieces
3 tbsp golden syrup
2 tbsp water

Chocolate & pear upside-down pudding

1 Grease and base-line a 25 cm/9 in deep, round, loose-bottomed cake tin. Preheat the oven to 180°C/350°F/Gas 4.

2 Melt 50 g/1³/₄ oz of the butter, mix with the demerara sugar and spread over the bottom of the cake tin.

3 Place an almond into each pear, then arrange the pears in the tin, cut side down and with stalk end toward the centre.

4 Cream the remaining butter with the caster sugar until light and fluffy. Beat in the eggs, 1 at a time, then fold in the flour, cocoa powder and ground almonds. If needed, add enough milk to form a soft dropping consistency. Spread the mixture evenly over the pears. Bake for 45–55 minutes or until the sponge springs back when lightly pressed.

5 To make the sauce, melt the chocolate with the syrup and water in a small heatproof bowl over a pan of simmering water, then beat until smooth. Turn the pudding out onto a serving dish, and pour over the warm chocolate sauce.

Makes 6
Prep time: 15 mins plus setting
Cook time: 14 mins

cocoa powder, for dusting
200 g/7 oz dark chocolate
(min.50–55% cocoa solids), broken
into pieces
150 g/5 oz butter, chopped + extra
for greasing

100 g/3½ oz caster sugar
3 eggs
3 egg yolks
1 tbsp dark rum (optional)
25 g/1 oz plain flour
whipped cream or icecream, to
serve

Chocolate fondant

1 Butter six 150 ml/5 fl oz dariole moulds well. Preheat the
oven to 200°C/400°F/Gas 6. Evenly coat the moulds with
sifted cocoa powder, tapping off any excess. Place the moulds
onto a baking sheet.

2 Gently heat together the chocolate, butter and sugar in a
heatproof bowl set over but not touching simmering water.
Once melted and the sugar no longer grainy, remove from the
heat and beat until smooth.

3 Add the eggs and egg yolks, one at a time, beating until
smooth and glossy. Add the rum if using and sift in the flour,
folding through gently.

4 Divide the mixture evenly between the moulds and place in
a fridge for at least 1 hour to set.

5 Cook for 14 minutes until risen and just setting on the
surface. Leave to stand for 2 minutes before carefully turning
out onto plates. Serve swiftly – with a generous dollop of
whipped cream or vanilla ice cream.

Serves 6
Prep time: 25 mins plus chilling
Cook time: 20 mins

4 eggs
75 g/2¾ oz caster sugar
25 g/1 oz ground walnuts
25 g/1 oz cocoa powder
25 g/1 oz plain flour
1–2 firm bananas

rum, to taste
300 ml/10 fl oz double cream
1 tbsp icing sugar

TO DECORATE
150 ml/5 fl oz double cream
50 g/1¾ oz dark chocolate (min. 50–55% cocoa solids), melted and cut into triangles, see page 11
2 tsp icing sugar

Chocolate, walnut & banana roulade

1 Line a 30 x 20 cm/12 x 8 in Swiss roll tin. Preheat the oven to 190°C/375°F/Gas 5.

2 Whisk the eggs and sugar in a large bowl until thick and creamy. Lightly fold in the walnuts, cocoa powder and flour. Spread the mixture gently and evenly into the tin. Cook for approximately 20 minutes or until the sponge is golden and springs back when pressed. Turn out onto a lightly floured kitchen paper, roll up and leave to cool.

3 Slice the bananas thinly, then sprinkle with a little rum. Whisk the cream and icing sugar until thick.

4 Neaten the edges of the sponge, then unroll and spread on the cream almost to the edges. Scatter on the bananas and re-roll. Wrap in cling-film and chill until ready to serve.

5 Whisk the double cream to soft peaks. Pipe the cream along the top of the roulade, decorate with the chocolate triangles and dust with icing sugar.

Serves 6
Prep time: 20 mins
Cook time: 10 mins

melted butter, for greasing
50 g/1¾ oz caster sugar + extra for dusting

175 g/6 oz dark chocolate (min. 50–55% cocoa solids) broken into pieces
3 tbsp double cream
4 egg yolks
5 egg whites
icing sugar, for dusting

Hot chocolate soufflé

1 You will need six 150 ml/5 fl oz ramekin dishes and one baking sheet. Preheat the oven to 200°C/400°F/Gas 6.

2 Place the baking sheet on the top shelf of the oven. Liberally brush the ramekin dishes with melted butter, sprinkle each with a teaspoon or so of the caster sugar, swirling to lightly coat, then tipping out excess.

3 Melt the chocolate and cream in a large heatproof bowl set over barely simmering water, cool, then whisk in the egg yolks.

4 Whisk the egg whites in another large clean bowl to soft peaks, then whisk in the remaining sugar, a little at a time until the egg whites are stiff. Whisk a spoonful into the chocolate mixture, then gently fold in the remaining egg whites.

5 Fill the ramekins, wipe the rims clean and run your thumb around the edges. This helps the soufflé rise evenly. Place the ramekins on the hot baking sheet and cook for 10–12 minutes or until risen and slightly wobbly.

6 Dust sieved icing sugar over the top, then serve straightaway.

Serves 8

Prep time: 30 mins

Cook time: 1–1 1/2 hours

75 g/2 3/4 oz pistachio nuts, coarsely chopped

5 egg whites

250 g/9 oz caster sugar

100 g/3 1/2 oz dark chocolate (min. 50–55% cocoa solids), chopped

100 g/3 1/2 oz good quality white chocolate, chopped

100 g/3 1/2 oz milk chocolate

450 ml/15 fl oz double cream

175 g/6 oz fresh raspberries

cocoa powder, for dusting

Triple chocolate pavlova

1 Line 2 baking sheets with baking parchment. Preheat the oven to 140°C/275°F/Gas 1. Draw a 23 cm/9 in circle on one sheet of parchment and a 15.5 cm/6 in circle on the other.

2 Dry-fry the nuts in a frying pan over a gentle heat. As soon as you smell a toasty aroma, remove from the heat to cool. Nuts burn very quickly!

3 Whisk the egg whites in a clean bowl until dry, then whisk in the sugar, a little at a time until glossy and stiff.

4 Gently fold in two-thirds of the nuts with the dark and white chocolate. Divide the meringue onto the parchment circles, spreading into peaked rounds. Bake for 1 1/2 hours or until dry and the base sounds hollow when lightly tapped. Turn off the oven leaving the meringues to cool in the oven.

5 Meanwhile make some chocolate curls or shavings with the milk chocolate, see page 11.

6 To serve, lightly whip the cream and spread two-thirds over the large meringue. Scatter on half of the fruit, then top with the small meringue. Spread the remaining cream on top, then scatter over the remaining fruit, the chocolate shavings, a scattering of nuts and finally a dusting of cocoa powder.

Makes 6

Prep time: 20 mins plus overnight chilling

600 ml/1 pt whipping cream
a few drops of vanilla extract

100 g/4 oz dark chocolate (min. 70–75 % cocoa solids), broken into pieces

6 large egg yolks

1 tsp cornflour

50 g/1¾ oz caster sugar + extra for sprinkling

Chocolate crème brûlée

1 You will need six 150 ml/5 fl oz ramekins.

2 Pour the cream into a non-stick saucepan, stir in the vanilla and heat gently until the cream is scalding. Add the chocolate and whisk until melted and smooth.

3 Meanwhile in a large bowl use a wooden spoon to blend together the egg yolks, cornflour and caster sugar until just mixed but not frothy. Continue stirring whilst gradually pouring the hot chocolate cream onto the eggs.

4 Return the custard mix to the saucepan and constantly stir heat over a gentle heat until the custard thickens. Do not allow it to boil. Dip the wooden spoon in the custard to coat the back of it then run your finger through. If the custard forms a parting it is ready.

5 Strain the chocolate custard into a jug, then pour into the ramekins. Place on a tray and cool before covering and refrigerating for 5–6 hours and preferably overnight.

6 Take the ramekins out of the fridge 2 hours before serving. Sprinkle on a thin layer of caster sugar, then use the blowtorch in sweeping movements to melt and caramelize the sugar. Alternatively, place the ramekins on a baking sheet under a hot grill until the sugar caramelizes.

Serves 6
Prep time: 10 mins
Cook time: 45–50 mins

100 g/3½ oz plain flour
2 level tsp baking powder

50 g/1¾ oz cocoa powder
150 g/5 oz granulated sugar
150 ml/5 fl oz single cream
a few drops of vanilla extract
75 g/2¾ oz demerara sugar
350 ml/12 fl oz boiling water

Puddle pudding

1 Lightly grease a 1.4 l/2½ pt ovenproof dish. Preheat the
oven oven to 160°C/325°F/Gas 3.

2 Sift the flour, baking powder and 2 tablespoons of the
cocoa powder into a bowl, then whisk in the granulated
sugar, cream and vanilla extract. Beat well to a smooth batter.

3 Pour into the dish. Mix together the remaining cocoa
powder with the demerara sugar and sprinkle evenly over the
surface. Pour on the boiling water.

4 Bake for 40–45 minutes or until risen, slightly moist but
firm to the touch. Divide between warm bowls, making sure
everyone gets a generous spoonful of the hidden hot
chocolate sauce.

TIP
Delicious with cold
pouring cream or
vanilla ice cream.

4

tarts & pies

Serves 8–10

Prep time: 15 mins plus chilling

Cook time: 50–60 mins

50 g/1³/₄ oz butter, melted

200 g/7 oz pack chocolate-coated or plain digestive biscuits, crushed

FILLING

150 g/5¹/₂ oz dark chocolate (min. 70–75% cocoa solids)

700 g/1lb 8 oz mascarpone cheese

125 g/4¹/₂ oz light soft brown sugar

2 tbsp cornflour

3 eggs, beaten

mini chocolate eggs, to decorate

WHITE CHOCOLATE SAUCE

125 g/4¹/₂ oz good quality white chocolate

125 ml/4 fl oz double cream

15 g/¹/₂ oz butter

Baked cheesecake with white chocolate sauce

1 Base-line a 23 cm/9 in non-stick, spring-form cake tin. Preheat the oven to 180°C/350°F/Gas 4.

2 Melt the butter in a large bowl over a pan of barely simmering water. Stir in the crushed biscuits, then spread into the tin, pressing down evenly. Chill for 5 minutes.

3 Melt the dark chocolate in a small heatproof bowl set over the pan of barely simmering water. Stir until smooth, remove from heat and leave to cool a little.

4 In a large bowl, whisk together the mascarpone, sugar and cornflour until smooth. Whisk in the cooled chocolate and eggs. Spread over the biscuit base and level. Bake for 50–60 minutes. Turn off the oven and leave the door ajar until the cheesecake is completely cool. Decorate with mini eggs.

5 To make the sauce, place the white chocolate and cream in a small heatproof bowl set over a pan of simmering water. Heat until melted, then whisk in the butter.

Serves 8–10
Prep time: 15 mins plus chilling
Cook time: 50–60 mins

100 g/3½ oz butter
250 g/9 oz plain shortbread or
digestive biscuits, crushed

FILLING
175 g/6 oz white chocolate
375 g/13 oz cream cheese

75 g/2¾ oz caster sugar
a few drops vanilla extract
3 large eggs
200 ml/7 fl oz soured cream

TOPPING
75 g/2¾ oz caster sugar
150 ml/5 fl oz water
450 g/1 lb mixed summer berries
8–10 mint leaves, torn

White chocolate cheesecake

1 Base-line a 20 cm/8 in spring-form cake tin. Preheat the
oven to 160°C/325°F/Gas 3.

2 Melt the butter in a bowl over a pan of barely simmering
water. Stir in the biscuit crumbs, then spread into the tin,
pressing down onto the base and sides. Chill for 5 minutes.

3 Melt the chocolate in a heatproof bowl over a pan of barely
simmering water, stirring until smooth. Remove from the heat.

4 Whisk the cream cheese with the sugar and vanilla until
smooth, then beat in the eggs, 1 at a time. Quickly stir the
soured cream into the melted chocolate and add to the cream
cheese mix, whisking until smooth. Pour over the biscuit base,
level and bake for 50–60 minutes. Leave at room temperature
for 1 hour, then chill until completely set.

5 For the topping, place the sugar and water in a pan and heat
gently until dissolved; bring to the boil and simmer for a few
minutes or until syrupy. Remove from the heat, then stir in
the fruit and half the mint leaves. Leave to cool, then chill.
Spoon over the cheesecake and decorate with remaining mint.

Serves 8–10

Prep time: 25 mins plus overnight soaking

Cook time: 33–45 mins

250 g/9 oz pitted ready-to-eat prunes, halved

3 tsp vanilla extract

175 g/6 oz butter

85 g/3 oz caster sugar

200 g/7 oz plain flour

50 g/1¾ oz cornflour

FILLING

100 g/3½ oz dark chocolate (min. 70–75% cocoa solids)

150 ml/5 fl oz double cream

2 tbsp caster sugar

250 g/9 oz mascarpone cheese

2 eggs, beaten

Dark chocolate, vanilla & prune tart

1 You will need a 23 cm/9 in deep fluted flan tin. Preheat the oven to 190°C/375°F/Gas 5.

2 Place the prunes in a bowl with the vanilla extract and 4 tbsp water. Stir to moisten thoroughly, then cover and leave in a cool place to soak overnight.

3 Cream the butter and sugar together, then work in both flours to a smooth firm dough. Place in the flan tin, pressing down evenly onto the base and sides. Chill for 15 minutes. Line the pastry case with greaseproof paper and fill with baking beans. Bake for 10–15 minutes, remove the beans and paper and bake for 3–5 minutes until just cooked. Reduce the oven temperature to 160°C/325°F/Gas 3.

4 Place the chocolate and cream in a heatproof bowl set over simmering water until the chocolate has just melted. Remove from the heat and whisk in the sugar, mascarpone and eggs.

5 Stir in the prunes and juices. Pour over the pastry case and bake for 20–25 minutes or until just set. Serve warm or chilled.

Makes 8
Prep time: 40 mins plus chilling
Cook time: 20 mins

250 g/9 oz plain flour
125 g/4½ oz salted butter, cubed
3 tbsp caster sugar

FILLING
400 ml/14 fl oz milk
1 vanilla pod, split lengthways
3 egg yolks
25 g/1 oz cornflour
200 g/7 oz white chocolate
2–3 tbsp redcurrant jelly
150 ml/5 fl oz whipping cream
225 g/8 oz fresh strawberries

Chocolate & strawberry tarts

1 You will need 8 x 9 cm/3½ in round fluted tartlet tins. Preheat the oven to 200°C/400°F/Gas 6.

2 Rub the flour and butter together in a bowl until they resemble breadcrumbs. Stir in the sugar; add 2–3 tbsp cold water and work together to a soft dough. Chill for 30 minutes.

3 Gently heat the milk and vanilla pod in a pan until just scalding. In a large bowl beat together the egg yolks and cornflour. Strain on the milk whisking all the time. Discard the pod. Return to the pan, break in half the white chocolate. Stir constantly over a gentle heat until the chocolate has melted and the custard thickened. Set aside until cool.

4 Cut the pastry into 6; roll each to circles large enough to line the tins. Trim any excess. Line with paper and baking beans; bake blind for 15 minutes. Remove the beans and paper and bake for another 5 minutes. Transfer to a wire rack to cool.

5 Melt the remaining chocolate in a heatproof bowl set over gently simmering water, then brush over the pastry cases. Melt the redcurrant jelly. Whisk the cream to soft peaks, then fold into the custard. Divide between the tarts, arrange the strawberries on top and drizzle over the redcurrant jelly. Chill.

Serves 8

Prep time: 15 mins plus chilling

Cook time: 43–60 mins

175 g/6 oz butter

85 g/3 oz caster sugar

200 g/7 oz plain flour

50 g/1³/4 oz cornflour

FILLING

200 g/7 oz dark chocolate
(min. 50–55% cocoa solids)

125 g/4¹/2 oz unsalted butter

1 tbsp instant coffee dissolved in
1 tbsp boiling water

150 ml/5 fl oz single cream

175 g/6 oz dark soft brown sugar

3 eggs, beaten

Mississippi mud pie

1 You will need a 23cm/9 in deep fluted flan tin. Preheat the
oven to 190°C/375°F/Gas 5.

2 Cream the butter and sugar together, then work in both
flours to a smooth, firm dough. Press into the flan tin, lining
it as evenly as possible. Chill for 15 minutes. Line the pastry
case with greaseproof paper and fill with baking beans. Bake
blind for 10–15 minutes, then remove the beans and paper
and return to the oven for 3–5 minutes until just cooked.
Reduce the oven temperature to 160°C/325°F/Gas 3.

3 Break the chocolate into a heatproof bowl set over gently
simmering water, adding the butter and coffee. Stir until the
chocolate has just melted. Remove from the heat and whisk in
the cream, dark sugar and eggs.

4 Pour into the pastry base and return to the oven for
30–40 minutes until the filling is set. Serve at room
temperature.

TIP

For an even richer filling,
replace the dark soft brown
sugar with muscovado
sugar.

Serves 8

Prep time: 20 mins plus chilling

75 g/2³/₄ oz butter

75 g/2³/₄ oz demerara sugar

175 g/6 oz chocolate oat biscuits, crushed

FILLING AND DECORATION

100 g/3¹/₂ oz dark chocolate (min. 70–75% cocoa solids)

4 tbsp rum

3 leaves gelatine

1 tbsp instant coffee granules dissolved in 5 tbsp boiling water

350 g/12 oz ricotta cheese

200 ml/7 fl oz whipping cream

3 eggs, separated

75 g/2³/₄ oz caster sugar

8 chocolate truffles , see page 53 (optional) and chocolate shavings

cocoa powder, to dust

Mocha rum cheesecake

1 You will need a 20 cm/8 in non-stick, spring-form cake tin.

2 Melt the butter in a pan over a low heat. Stir in the sugar and crushed biscuits and mix well. Spread into the cake tin, pressing down evenly. Chill for 5 minutes.

3 Melt the chocolate in a small heatproof bowl set over a pan of barely simmering water, Stir in the rum, then remove from heat and leave to cool a little.

4 Soak the gelatine in a bowl of cold water for 5 minutes, then squeeze out the excess liquid, Place the coffee in a small bowl, add the gelatine and whisk until dissolved. In a large bowl, whisk together the ricotta cheese, cream, egg yolks and sugar until smooth. Whisk in the coffee mixture and the cooled chocolate.

5 Whisk the egg whites in a bowl until softly peaking. Whisk a spoonful into the cheese mixture, then gently fold in the rest. Pour onto the biscuit base and chill for 4–6 hours minimum. Run a palette knife around the edge of the tin, then release the spring clip and slide onto a serving plate. Decorate with truffles if liked and chocolate curls and dust with cocoa powder.

Recipe index

ACKNOWLEDGEMENT

The author would like to thank the photographer, Michael Prior, for always going that
extra mile – www.michaelpriorphotographer.com